Finding the Still Point

DHARMA COMMUNICATIONS BOOKS

by John Daido Loori

Cave of Tigers
Modern Zen Encounters

Celebrating Everyday Life
Zen Home Liturgy

Hearing with the Eye
Photographs from Point Lobos

Invoking Reality
Moral and Ethical Teachings of Zen

Making Love with Light
Contemplating Nature with Words and Photographs

Mountain Record of Zen Talks

Finding the Still Point
A Beginner's Guide to Zen Meditation

Teachings of the Earth
Zen and the Environment

Two Arrows Meeting in Mid-Air
The Zen Koan

Finding the Still Point

A Beginner's Guide
to Zen Meditation

JOHN DAIDO LOORI

SHAMBHALA • *Boston & London* • 2007

Shambhala Publications, Inc.
Horticultural Hall
300 Massachusetts Avenue
Boston, Massachusetts 02115
www.shambhala.com

9 8 7 6 5 4 3 2 1

First Shambhala Edition
Designed by Lora Zorian
Printed in Singapore

♾This edition is printed on acid-free paper that meets
the American National Standards Institute z39.48 Standard.
Distributed in the United States by Random House, Inc.,
and in Canada by Random House of Canada Ltd

See page 113 for Library of Congress cataloging-in-
publication data

Contents

Part Two

A DHARMA DISCOURSE

PART ONE

The Practice
of Zen Meditation

WHAT IS *ZAZEN?*

THERE ARE MANY SCHOOLS of Buddhism and a vast array of teachings on how to realize our true nature. Some schools focus on the rules of conduct. Others concentrate on academic study and debate. Still others use visualizations and chanting of sacred sounds and words. In Zen, the emphasis is on *zazen*, or sitting Zen. Zazen is the heart of the Zen path.

To practice zazen is to study the self. In its early stages, zazen has the appearance of what is normally called meditation. But we should understand that zazen is more than just meditation. It is not mere contemplation or introspection. It is not quieting the mind or focusing the mind. Zazen is sitting Zen—one aspect of Zen. There is also walking Zen, working Zen, laughing Zen, and crying Zen. Zen is a way of using one's mind and living one's life, and doing this with other people. No rule book has ever been written that can adequately describe Zen. You have to go very deep into yourself to find its foundations.

The great Zen Master Eihei Dogen said,

> *To study the Buddha Way is to study the self,*
> *To study the self is to forget the self,*

To forget the self is to be enlightened by the
ten thousand things.

To study the self is zazen. To forget the self is zazen. To be enlightened by the ten thousand things is zazen—it is to recognize the unity of the self and the whole phenomenal universe.

The Buddha attained enlightenment while practicing a form of seated meditation. Zen practice constantly returns to that basic seated form. This practice has continued for twenty-five hundred years, transmitted from realized practitioner to realized practitioner, from generation to generation. It traveled from India to China, from China to Korea and Japan, and in the twentieth century it arrived in the West.

Zazen is a very simple practice. It is very easy

to describe and very easy to follow. But like all practices, it takes "doing" in order for anything to happen. And what happens with zazen can transform our lives.

Most of us spend our time preoccupied. We are constantly carrying on an internal dialogue. While we are involved in talking to ourselves, we miss the moment-to-moment awareness of our life. We look, but we don't see. We listen, but we don't hear. We eat, but we don't taste. We love, but we don't feel. The senses are receiving all the information, but because of our preoccupations, cognition is not taking place. Zazen brings us back to each moment. The moment is where our life takes place. If we miss the moment we miss our life.

Every other creature on the face of the earth seems to know how to be quiet and still.

A butterfly on a leaf; a cat in front of a fireplace; even a hummingbird comes to rest sometime. But humans are constantly on the go. We seem to have lost the ability to just be quiet, to simply be present in the stillness that is the foundation of our lives. Yet if we never get in touch with that stillness, we never fully experience our lives.

When the mind is at rest, the body is at rest—respiration, heartbeat, and metabolism slow down. Reaching this still point is not something unusual or esoteric. It is a very important part of being alive and staying awake. All creatures on the earth are capable of manifesting this stillness.

In zazen, as you practice letting go of your thoughts and internal dialogue, and bringing your mind back to the breath, the breath will slowly get easier and deeper, and the mind will naturally rest. The mind is like the surface of a pond. When the wind blows, the surface is disturbed. Then there are waves and ripples, and the image of the sun or the moon or whatever the surface is reflecting is broken up.

When the wind quiets down, the surface of the pond becomes like glass. The stilled mind is like a mirror. It doesn't process, it just reflects. When there is a flower in front of it, it reflects a flower. When the flower is gone, the reflection is gone. When a fire engine goes by, we hear the fire engine. When the fire engine is gone, its reflection is gone. The mind returns to that original smooth surface. A still mind is unobstructed—always open and receptive. It doesn't hold on or attach to anything. At any moment in time, it is free.

2

POSITIONING
THE BODY

I N STARTING THE PRACTICE of zazen, the
first thing you need to do is find a correct sitting position for the body. Your posture greatly
influences what happens with your breath and
your mind, so it is important to pay meticulous
attention to how you position yourself for zazen.
During the twenty-five-hundred-year evolution

of Buddhism, the most stable and powerful position found for the practice of zazen has been the pyramidal structure of the seated Buddha.

Sit on a *zafu,* a small meditation pillow (to raise your buttocks and to help your knees touch the ground). With your bottom on the pillow and your two knees against the ground, the body forms a tripod, with a base that provides great stability. The spine is erect—not stiff and not slumped. Your torso is perpendicular to the floor—not leaning to the right or left, forward or backward. Your head rests squarely atop your spine, not tilting in any direction. You should wear loose clothing when sitting, so your circulation is free and the breathing movements of your rib cage and lower abdomen are not constricted.

Cross-Legged Postures

There are several different leg positions that you can assume while seated on the floor. The simplest one, requiring the least joint flexibility, is the Burmese position (fig. 1).

In the Burmese posture the right foot is drawn up close to the thigh, allowing the foot and calf to rest on the floor or sitting mat. The left foot is placed in front of the right calf so that both knees touch the mat. The reverse position (i.e., with the left foot drawn up to the thigh and the right foot placed in front) can also be adopted. If your knees don't reach the floor, consider using a zafu with more loft. If this doesn't help, you might consider placing support cushions under your knees. Don't sit squarely in the middle of the zafu; instead, use it as a wedge

FIGURE 1. Burmese position.

under your buttocks, with only the forward third actually supporting you. This adjustment will distribute your weight more equally between the three points of the tripod (your bottom and your knees), relieving some of the strain on your back.

The next position is the half lotus (fig. 2). In this position the right leg is tucked under the left thigh. The left foot is then placed on the right thigh. Because one foot is up on the thigh while the other foot is under the thigh, the body tends to tilt slightly to one side. This must be compensated for very carefully when you are centering yourself by positioning the zafu so that it supports the opposite buttock. To balance out this position, try reversing your legs every other time you sit; instead of having the left foot up and the right foot under, put the right foot up and the left foot under.

FIGURE 2. Half lotus position.

By far the most stable of all of the positions is the full lotus (fig. 3). This is a perfectly symmetrical and stable posture. Assuming the full lotus position is difficult, if not impossible, for a beginner, mostly due to tightness in the leg muscles. With steady practice, however, the muscles loosen up considerably. Once you have seated yourself on the zafu, place your right foot on your left thigh and the left foot on the right thigh. As before, the reverse position is also possible. Make sure that your heels are drawn up as close to your abdomen as possible. The soles of both feet should point at the ceiling.

Kneeling Position

When sitting in kneeling position, or *seiza* (fig. 4), the zafu is turned on its side and placed between your heels. This arrangement keeps the weight

FIGURE 3. Full lotus position.

FIGURE 4. Kneeling position.

of your body off your feet. Remember that the basic model for your sitting posture is a pyramid, so keep your knees far enough apart to create a broad, firm base. You can also use a specially designed tilted sitting bench to keep all the weight off your feet, allowing you to maintain an erect spine with very little effort.

Sitting in a Chair

Somehow people feel reluctant about practicing zazen in a chair, as though it were less authentic or spiritual than sitting on the floor with legs crossed. There is absolutely no esoteric significance to sitting cross-legged on the floor. A chair is stable, solid, and enables the whole body to relax with a minimal amount of muscle tension, so you can sit easily without worrying about toppling over. That is its importance. Ultimately,

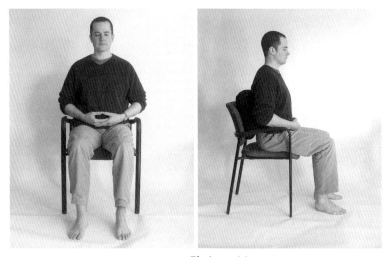

FIGURE 5. Chair position.

the significance of zazen is what you do with your mind, not what you do with your feet or your legs.

Thus there is no reason why you can't sit effectively in a chair (fig. 5), either temporarily until you get in shape for floor sitting, or permanently if your age, physique, or condition requires it. When using a chair, it's good to place a zafu on the seat. Sit on the forward third of the cushion and try to keep your feet flat on the floor. Support your body with the strength of your spine, without external props. The temptation when sitting in a chair is to slouch and rest against the chair-back. This creates a tendency toward lazy and sleepy sitting.

Again, in this position, as in all the other positions, taking meticulous care of your posture allows the skeletal structure to hold the body upright without unnecessary tension and strain. Thus, the body will relax, becoming soft and pliable. Coupled with deep, even, natural breathing, these seated postures help the blood vessels, nerves, and other organs of the body to function freely, improving health and vitality.

3

CENTERING
THE BODY

O NCE YOU HAVE ASSUMED a sitting position, whether on the floor with legs
crossed, kneeling, or on a chair, you need to center your spine. Begin by gently rocking in large
arcs from side to side. Don't let your head move
independently, but keep it as an extension of your
spine, so that the breathing passages are always
aligned and completely open. If you are sitting

cross-legged, when swaying, keep your knees firmly planted on the floor. Start with wide arcs, slowly letting their size naturally decrease as your momentum diminishes, until you just drift to a stop. If you can avoid controlling the rate of speed and duration of the swings, you become a plumb bob that naturally comes to rest in a position perpendicular to the floor. In doing this, you are allowing the center of your body to declare itself.

The next step is to elongate the spine. Imagine that the ceiling is resting on the crown of your head at a point directly over your spine. Let your spine begin to extend, from its base upward, lifting the head with it as it straightens. Feel that thrust lift the ceiling. Let your spine do the lifting. In the lumbar region of the back, the lower back, there will be a slight curve so that your stomach pushes out slightly. Now relax, but don't let the spine cave in.

Balanced sitting is mostly a matter of getting arranged properly. Keeping upright is only an effort if you are using your back muscles to remain erect by brute force. If you develop back pain, it's a signal that you aren't sitting in a way that is balanced. Pay attention to any discomfort you feel when sitting and let it teach you about your posture.

4

HEAD AND HANDS

WHEN DOING ZAZEN your mouth is closed. Unless you have nasal blockage you should breathe through your nose. The tongue is pressed lightly against the upper palate. This slows down the amount of salivation so you don't have to swallow repeatedly. The eyes are lowered, gazing at the ground about three feet in front of you. The chin is slightly tucked in. Although the zazen posture looks very disciplined, the body and muscles should be soft, with no tension in the body.

The hands are held in what we call the *cosmic mudra* (fig. 6). The active hand is held palm up and it holds the inactive hand. This means if you are right-handed, your right hand is holding the left hand. If you are left-handed, your left hand is holding the right hand. The middle knuckles overlap and the thumb-tips touch lightly, forming an oval frame. If you are sitting in the full lotus position, your heels form a natural base to support the backs of your hands. If you are sitting in one of the other positions, you may find that your hands are not symmetrically arranged and supported, or that your shoulders get sore from the strain of holding up your arms during meditation. Rather than trying to place your hands in some ideal position, simply let them rest naturally in your lap, as you form the cosmic mudra.

FIGURE 6. Cosmic mudra.

5

THE *HARA*

THE *HARA* is a point two or three fingers' breadth below the navel. It roughly corresponds to the physical center of the body and its center of gravity. In Zen it is considered to be the spiritual center of the body. While doing zazen, place your attention there.

In the West, we have a tendency to focus our attentiveness in our face, as that's what we show and project to the world. We are always aware of

our face. When we do something embarrassing, blood immediately rushes to our face, and it turns red. As your zazen matures, the hara will naturally become the center of your attentiveness. You will walk from the hara, work from the hara, and when you get embarrassed, you will have a warm hara instead of a red face. Little by little, the hara will become the focus of power in your body. When something unusual or unexpected happens, rather than feeling scattered, you will find that energy will automatically concentrate in the hara. You will have discovered the still point out of which comes all the activity of your life.

6

BREATHING

BREATH IS LIFE. The word *spirit* means breath. The words *ki* in Japanese and *chi* in Chinese, meaning power or energy, both derive from breath. Breath is the key to zazen. It is the vital force in our bodies. In zazen you will discover how breathing and posture are closely allied to your emotions. Notice how when your mind is agitated, your breath is agitated. Discover how anger, for instance, affects the depth and rate of your breathing. Check your body to see where your muscles are tense. Notice if your posture is unbalanced, your jaw clenched, or shoulders hunched. When your mind is at rest, breathing is deep and easy, without effort.

In working with the breath you are automatically working with the body and mind. Body, breath, and mind are one reality. We tend to see them separately, but in zazen they unify and we experience their interpenetration directly. In sitting and in daily life, try to return to an open, balanced posture and full, even breathing. As you recognize and consciously influence your posture and breathing patterns, you will discover within yourself more patience, calm, and emotional stability. Such equanimity is an asset that imparts tremendous strength.

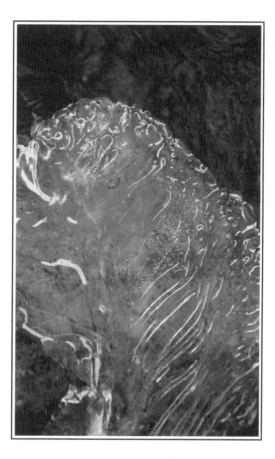

Whichever zazen posture you use, try to relax the abdominal muscles and let the lower belly work like a bellows, expanding with inhalation and contracting with exhalation. Try not to move the belly consciously; instead, let the volume of air move it. This is the way infants naturally breathe.

Breathe softly. Do not overfill or empty the lungs to the point of strain, nor hold your breath. The inhalations should be effortless. Just let go, and your lungs will naturally refill by themselves. Deep, natural breathing can't be forced. It occurs spontaneously once you take the right posture, positioning your body properly.

7

RELAXATION
EXERCISE

I F YOU ARE entirely new to Zen practice and unfamiliar with the zazen postures described earlier, before you begin to concentrate on the breath, there is a short relaxation process you can use as a way of settling your body and mind.

Begin by taking one of the zazen postures, making sure that your posture is balanced. The eyes are lowered and mouth is closed. You are breathing through your nose. Focus your awareness on the muscles around the eyes. Be aware of any tension that may be there, and then deliberately and consciously let all the tension go. Now turn your awareness to the muscles of the jaw. Feel any tension there and deliberately and consciously let it go. Next, the muscles of the shoulders and the neck, and those of the arms, forearms, and hands. Be aware of any tension that may be held in these areas and deliberately and consciously let it go.

Become aware of the muscles of the back. Let go of any tension there, then move your attention to the chest, letting go of any tension there. Feel your breath. It should be deep and easy. Imagine each inhalation bringing energy into the body and each exhalation releasing all tension. Become aware of your thigh muscles and release

any tension there. Now the muscles of the calves, the tendons in the feet. Consciously release the tension.

Return your awareness to the breath. Taste the breath. Be aware of the tactile sensation of breathing. Feel the coolness of an inhalation in the back of your throat. Feel the warmth of the exhalation. If your mind begins to wander, watch what it is doing. Acknowledge the thoughts, let them go, and bring your attentiveness back to the breath—tasting, feeling, experiencing it.

8

COUNTING
THE BREATH

ZAZEN PRACTICE BEGINS with counting the breath, counting each inhalation and each exhalation. You count "one" on the inhalation and "two" on the exhalation, counting up to ten. When you get to ten, come back to one and start all over again.

As you do this, make an agreement with yourself. If your mind begins to wander and you are chasing thoughts, once you notice you are distracted, acknowledge the thought, let it go, and return to the count of "one." Each time you acknowledge a thought and release it, you are empowering yourself with the ability to put your mind where you want it, when you want it, for as long as you want it there. That simple activity is extremely powerful.

Random thoughts will continue to occur. They are the natural activity of a healthy mind and are not a problem in sitting. If you tried to stop these random thoughts you would fall into a trance state, which is not what zazen is about. But becoming engrossed in imaginary story lines or discursive thoughts is a distraction. Then, you are not practicing zazen. You are thinking.

A possible scenario runs like this. You are sitting, counting your breath when, at the count of "four," you suddenly hear a fire engine go by. The instant you hear its siren, a whole chain of thoughts is set in motion:

> I wonder whose house it is? Since it's going up the street, the fire must be up that way. I'll bet it's the third house on the right. I knew that house was going to catch fire, it's an obvious fire trap. God, I hope those kids who were playing outside are safe. Isn't it awful that people don't take care of their homes . . .

Before you know it, you have developed a full-blown story. You are a thousand miles away from your breath and posture, totally involved in this self-created, imaginary drama. When you realize what you are doing, acknowledge your thoughts,

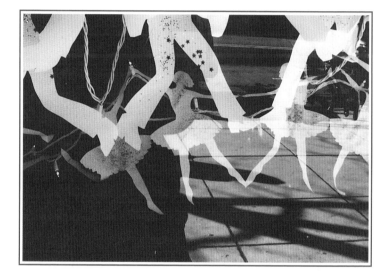

deliberately release them, and bring your attention back to the breath, starting the count again at "one."

There are times when something important has come up in your life or you are in a crisis, and you find that when you let go of a thought it will reoccur. You let go of the thought; it comes back. You let it go, and it comes back again. If that happens, engage the thought, really see it, be aware of any feelings associated with it. Allow it to run its course to exhaustion. But watch it. Be aware of it. When the process feels complete, release it, come back to the breath, and start again at "one." Don't use zazen to suppress thoughts or emotions that need to come up to your consciousness. Similarly, do not suppress thoughts of pain or discomfort. Thoughts will come up that you need to deal with. That's not a failure.

Treating your thoughts in this open manner is another way of practicing.

In the early stages of your practice, you may think that you are becoming more distracted than ever. It may seem that no matter how strongly you concentrate on your breath, you are unable to get beyond the count of "two" without the mind voicing an opinion or judgment. Your thoughts are not increasing; you are simply hearing your incessant internal chatter for the first time.

We constantly talk to ourselves! It is this scattering of mental activity that keeps us separated from one another, from our environment and, indeed, from ourselves. Most people find that many weeks or even months of practice are necessary before the count of "ten" is reached for the first time without being distracted by thoughts. In the process of getting there you will begin to notice many things you never noticed before. They were always there, but because of your preoccupations—that incessant internal dialogue—you were too busy to see what was happening within you and around you.

Once you are able to stay with the counting and repeatedly get to "ten" without any effort, you can start counting every cycle of the breath. Inhalation and exhalation would count as "one," the next inhalation and exhalation as "two," and so on. This provides less feedback, but as time goes on you need less feedback because you can focus on the breath more easily, and, in general, your mind is quieter.

Eventually, as your mind settles down and your concentration deepens, you can just follow the breath, abandoning the counting altogether.

Just be with the breath. Just *be* the breath. Let the breath breathe itself. That's the beginning of the experience of the falling away of body and mind or *samadhi*. Samadhi is the single-pointedness of mind, a state of being in which the mind stops analyzing, judging, categorizing.

This whole process takes time. You shouldn't rush it. Don't move too fast from counting every breath, to counting cycles of breath, to following the breath. If you go from one stage to another prematurely, you will not develop strong concentration, true one-pointedness of mind. It is important to be patient and persistent, allowing stillness and clarity to ripen and emerge organically. Each step along the way is the "real thing," and the progression from counting the breath to following the breath should not be thought of in terms of spiritual progress or achievement.

9

WALKING
MEDITATION

WALKING MEDITATION, or *kinhin*, is moving meditation. Although zazen is the heart of our practice, it is also important for us to learn to make the transition from the stillness of seated meditation into movement and activity while maintaining the same degree of concentration. Walking meditation helps us to practice just that.

FIGURE 7. Walking meditation.

When you have finished a meditation period, prepare to stand by first rocking your body from side to side. Slowly unfold your legs and come to your feet. Place your hands in the *shashu* mudra: making a fist with your left hand at the level of your hara, cover it lightly with your right hand. As in zazen, your eyes should remain lowered in order to minimize distractions (fig. 7).

During walking meditation, stay centered in your hara. Keep your breathing slow and even, as this will help you to remain grounded. Take one full breath—inhale, and as you finish exhaling, take one small half step forward, placing all of your attention on the act of walking. Inhale, exhale, take another half step. When thoughts arise, see them, let them go, and return to just walking. Continue doing slow kinhin for a minute or two, then move into fast kinhin. Keep in mind that this is a relaxed, natural walk. It should not feel either rushed or sluggish. Kinhin is not a break, and it is not exercise. It is practice.

If you've sat for a period of thirty minutes, ten minutes of walking meditation makes a good balance. Kinhin, like zazen, appears to be a very easy practice, but very few of us ever really do it. It is easy to say "just walk," but it is difficult to do. The key is to give yourself to it completely. When you walk, just walk. When you sit, just sit. This is what it means to be awake. This is how you give life to the Buddha.

10

HOME PRACTICE

ZAZEN IS AN IMPORTANT PART of your life, as important as breathing, eating, and sleeping. The best way to do it is to fit it into your daily routine. The key is continuity and consistency. Do it every day—ten minutes in the morning, ten minutes at night. Make an agreement with yourself to sit each day for a set period of time. It is much more beneficial to sit consistently for ten or fifteen minutes every day than to sit for two or three hours every now and then. You can use zazen as a way of entering the day in the morning and letting go of the day as you get ready to go to sleep.

Zazen is best practiced at the beginning and end of each day, as these times are usually quiet and free of interruption. Get up in the morning, wash your face, brush your teeth, do zazen, have breakfast, take a shower, get dressed, go to work. Once zazen becomes part of the daily routine you can do it with ease.

Find a place to sit that can be left undisturbed. It can be the corner of the room, a closet, or an entire room if you have a lot of space available. Wherever it is, maintain it as a place for zazen practice. In this way that space will become a sacred space for you. To reflect clarity and tranquillity, it should be neat, attractive and without distractions.

You may want to set up a little altar. It doesn't need to be a Buddhist altar. If you are a Christian, you can have a Christian altar. If you are Jewish, you can have a special area with a candle and a bowl for incense. This area becomes the center of the sacred space. A stick of incense can be burned to measure each sitting period, so you don't need to continually consult a conventional timepiece during your sitting.

Little by little, day by day, your practice will deepen, revealing a mind that is open, free, and receptive. The more we sit zazen, the more we come in contact with our lives and the way our minds work. We will never find complete and lasting peace in this life until we realize personally

the inherent perfection of our own life, an inherent freedom that all of us are born with.

From birth we have been conditioned by different events and people—our teachers, parents, country, culture, neighborhood, friends, and peers. Everything we cherish—our positions, attitudes, opinions, all of our attachments, all the things we think give our life identity—is found in our conditioning. Now here we are, decades later, trying to live our lives out of this random programming we call "my life." We feel so strongly about parts of the program we are ready to die for it. And it is all created in our own mind.

There is no escaping the fact that getting beyond this accumulated conditioning is a long process. Thirty or forty years of programming takes time to work through. We look at the thoughts, acknowledge them, let them go, and come back to the breath. Day by day, we uncover what is underneath all of the conditioning. What we discover is called freedom. It is called human life. It is called wisdom and compassion. It's the nature of all beings.

This inherent nature is the spiritual fire that brings us to ask questions, to probe, to sit zazen. It keeps us from being satisfied with pat answers and platitudes. We don't need a rule book to go by. We've come into this life fully equipped as a buddha, an awakened being, and we'll go out fully equipped as a buddha, realized or not. Some will realize it, some will not, and whether we do or don't is up to each one of us. It depends on how much we are willing to practice our life, how willing we are to search deeply enough to realize it directly.

Once realized, all the questions dissolve. Differences merge and a whole new reality, a whole new way of understanding ourselves and the universe begins to develop. Reading this book is a drop in the ocean, a beginning. If you use that drop, practice that drop, then it will eventually be the ocean that covers the earth, encompasses the heavens, reaching everywhere, touched by everything. That is your life.

PART TWO

A Dharma Discourse

INTRODUCTION

A DHARMA DISCOURSE, or *teisho,* is a formal talk on a significant aspect of the Zen teachings. It is not an intellectual presentation or philosophical explanation, but a direct expression of the spirit of Zen by the teacher to his or her students.

Dharma discourses generally deal with a Zen koan—a seemingly paradoxical statement or question that challenges our understanding of who we are, what the nature of the self is, and what the activity of our life expresses. There are many texts with commentaries on classical Zen koans by both Eastern and Western teachers currently available in English. These texts provide access to the way Zen study has been brought to life through the lineage of realized teachers that began with Shakyamuni Buddha twenty-five hundred years ago.

Dharma discourses are said to be "dark to the mind but radiant to the heart." They require that we open ourselves to what initially may appear to be an intentionally confusing and frustrating way of using language. At Zen Mountain Monastery, dharma discourses are offered following the community's formal sitting periods, but they are received with the same spirit and focus that we have during zazen. Receiving the dharma discourse in this way allows the words to flow freely through us, and works to open the center of our being.

Because reading is essentially solitary, the intimacy of heart-to-heart, mind-to-mind communication that characterizes dharma discourses may be even more accessible to you as a reader. Please read the words that follow with your heart and give them your full attention, letting go of all the thoughts and analysis that are part of our habitual way of using our minds.

The practice of reading or hearing a dharma discourse does not involve acquiring information, but instead lies in the direct and personal experience of the awakened mind. Our job is to get out of our own way, so that we can experience what has always been present within each and every one of us.

THE GREAT WAY

THE GREAT WAY *is not difficult;*
It only avoids picking and choosing.
When love and hate are both absent,
Everything becomes clear and undisguised.
Make the smallest distinction, however,
And heaven and earth are set
   infinitely apart.

If you wish to see the truth,
Then hold no opinions for or against
anything.
To set up what you like against what
you dislike
Is a disease of the mind.
When the deep meaning of things is not
understood,
The mind's essential peace is disturbed to
no avail.
The Way is perfect like vast space,
Where nothing is lacking and nothing
is in excess.
Indeed, it is due to our choosing to accept
or reject
That we do not see the true nature of things.
Live neither in the entanglements of
outer things

Nor in inner feelings of emptiness.
Be serene in the oneness of things
And such erroneous views will disappear
  by themselves.
To deny the reality of things
Is to miss their reality;
To assert the emptiness of things
Is to miss their reality.
The more you talk and think about it,
The further astray you wander from
  the truth.
Stop talking and thinking
And there is nothing that you will not be
  able to know.

This passage is from *The Faith Mind Sutra: Verses on the Unfailing Source of Life* by Master Sengcan (J. Sozan). It deals with faith in mind, faith in how the mind really functions. Later in the sutra, Master Sengcan says:

> *One thing, all things,*
> *Move among and intermingle without*
>   *distinction.*
> *To live in this realization,*
> *Is to be without anxiety about nonperfection;*
> *To live in this faith is the road to nonduality,*
> *Because the nondual is one with a trusting*
>   *mind.*

One thing, all things, move among and intermingle without distinction points to the unfailing source of life that Sengcan mentions in the subtitle. It refers to the metaphor of the Diamond Net of Indra. Everything throughout space and time is interconnected, and at each connection—

at each point—is a diamond that reflects every other diamond, so that in this vast net, each diamond contains every other diamond. This is one thing, all things, moving among and intermingling without distinction. The diamond net is "the unfailing source of life." Indeed, it is life itself, your life itself. We separate ourselves from this unfailing source of life with our mind, our thoughts, our ideas. But the only way you can separate yourself is mentally, because *one thing, all things, move among and intermingle* is the way it is, whether we realize it or not. Regardless of whether we live our lives according to this understanding or not, the fact remains that it is the way things are. With our minds we separate ourselves and immediately create all the dualities of life. On one side we create pain, greed, anger—fundamental ignorance. We also create

the other side—joy, compassion, wisdom, and enlightenment.

When love and hate are both absent, everything becomes clear and undisguised. When duality is absent, everything becomes clear. But we shouldn't cling to this "clarity" either. The other side of clarity is confusion; both are diseases of the mind. All of the dualities are mutually arising; they are all codependent. You can't have one without the other: good and bad, heads and tails, heaven and earth. That is why it is said, *Make the smallest distinction, . . . and heaven and earth are set infinitely apart.* They are not set apart until we separate them in our minds (and by "we" I do not mean only Westerners—the same thing holds true of people in China, Japan, India, and every place else). Civilization itself is founded on the dualistic use of the mind. The

Buddha went beyond dualism, beyond the distinction between this and that, to show that there is no self, that what we call the "self" is a creation of our own consciousness, which separates us from everything else.

Picking and choosing, coming and going, love and hate, inside and outside, having and not having, accepting and rejecting, asserting and denying, form and emptiness, right and wrong— they all begin with making the smallest distinction. They all begin with the idea of a separate self, a boundary between the self and the rest of reality, an inside and an outside. Coming and going is such a difficult and painful process. Our lives are filled with the pains of coming and going: coming into a relationship, a marriage, a new job, a new place; leaving a relationship, a marriage, a job, the place where you live. We do not seem to understand how to execute these life functions without creating pain, anger, or confusion. We are tearing ourselves away from some imaginary thing that we stick to—that by its very nature cannot be stuck to or torn away from. Coming is always right here and right now. Going is always right here and right now. It is because there is no coming and no going that we can speak of coming and going.

Because of that illusion of separateness, we find it hard to come and go. We find it difficult to come together, difficult to part. I know many people who have had wonderful relationships, but because of the time, the circumstances, or various changes in their lives, they have had to go their separate ways. To be able to do that, somehow the creation of anger is usually necessary. There is that need to feel justified, to have a reason to separate. Since love is what brings us together—that is our rationale—then hate must be what will drive us apart. So we create anger. It is unnecessary, and so poisonous. Coming and going is a functioning of life, like waves rising and falling. We can learn to come and go without coming and going. We can learn to avoid picking and choosing. So how can we avoid picking and choosing, coming and going? Just to open our mouths to speak is picking and choosing. Just to say "avoid picking and choosing" is picking and choosing. What kind of practice avoids picking and choosing? Avoids coming and going?

This suffering, this picking and choosing, this painful coming and going, is related to ignorance. Master Sengcan says, *It is due to our choosing to accept or reject that we do not see the true nature of things.* Later in the sutra, he tells us, *The changes that appear to occur in the empty world we call real only because of our ignorance.* Ignorance means not knowing what is real. It is very easy to get totally lost in the confusion between the apparent and real. In a way, our lives are based on that confusion, on our fundamental assumption of a separate self, an assumption that is simply false. The consequence of this basic premise, and all the delusive thoughts that arise from it, is suffering in its multitude of forms. The practice that avoids picking and choosing, coming and going, is the practice that avoids dualism, that brings us back to the ground of our being.

The great Master Joshu very often used this *Faith Mind Sutra* of Master Sozan to teach his monks. One day a monk asked him: "It is said that the Great Way is not difficult; it only avoids picking and choosing. Now, what is not picking and choosing?" Zhaozhou said, "I alone am holy throughout heaven and earth." The monk responded, "That is still picking and choosing." And Zhaozhou said: "Asshole! Where's the picking and choosing?" The monk was speechless.

Zhaozhou answered him with the words of the Buddha: "I alone am the Honored One between heaven and earth." He is saying there is nothing outside of me; I am the Diamond Net of Indra. In a sense, that is picking and choosing, but only when you are coming from a position other than the position Zhaozhou was standing in. The monk was standing outside of that, and from his point of view he was justified in saying "that is still picking and choosing." Position is everything. Everything changes, even when the circumstances remain identical, when you shift your position. Try it sometime with someone

who is an adversary. Shift your position. Be that person, and the adversary disappears. Shift positions with whatever barrier you are facing in zazen, in your life. Be the barrier, and it is no longer there. It is only there because we pull back, separate ourselves from it. The more we pull back, the bigger and more overwhelming it gets, and the angrier or the more frightened we become. If we really look at the anger that makes us crazy, or the fear that stops us cold, we see that it develops step by step from our thought process. And the starting point of that thought process is separation. Is the cause of the fear something that might be lurking in a dark alley? The possibility of falling down and breaking your neck? Losing your job? No, it is yourself. When you really acknowledge that it is nothing but yourself, when you realize this fact, you cannot live your life in the old way. You've suddenly taken responsibility for it. Before, the problem was outside—your bad luck, what others did to you, the circumstances you could do nothing about.

When you realize that the cause is you, you empower yourself. You suddenly become a ten-thousand-foot-high buddha—you fill the universe. There is no picking and choosing, coming or going—no place to go, no place to come from. Zhaozhou was trying to show the monk that ten-thousand-foot-high buddha. But the monk was standing in a different position. So Zhaozhou yelled, "Asshole!" Actually the Chinese word is usually translated as "country bumpkin" or "stupid oaf," but this sounds too tame for our ears. It was meant to shock, to stun the monk into experiencing the reality of what the Buddha said: "I alone am the Honored

One between heaven and earth!" Nothing is outside of you.

Joshu was coming from the position of the absolute, which would become a kind of blindness if he stuck there. But when the monk said, "That is still picking and choosing," Joshu shouted, "Asshole! Where's the picking and choosing?" immediately shifting positions, slamming right into that monk from the relativistic standpoint. He was showing him: you and I are the same thing, but I am not you and you are not me. We should not stick anywhere—not in the relative, not in the absolute.

> *To deny the reality of things*
> *Is to miss their reality;*
> *To assert the emptiness of things*
> *Is to miss their reality.*

Sticking to clarity, to enlightenment, is the worst kind of delusion. In Zen there is going beyond clarity. As Zen Master Dogen says, "No trace of enlightenment remains and this traceless enlightenment continues endlessly." Going beyond clarity, not abiding in it, is very ordinary. There is no stink of Zen about it, no holiness to hold on to.

In the vast Diamond Net of Indra, each thing contains everything, and each thing is separate and distinct from everything else. Thinking, talking, and doing are the ways we create our lives, the ways we create our karma. We can see how our actions create causes, and we can see that every cause has consequences. The same is true for our thought. It is because of our interconnectedness, our intermingling and moving among this one thing, that it works in that way.

Because of that, talking and thinking and doing can create karma. We can use karma to poison or to nourish, depending upon how we manifest it. How do we manifest it so that it nourishes, so that it heals? By nontalking, nonthinking, nondoing. How do you do nonthinking and nondoing? How can you possibly avoid picking and choosing?

> *The more you talk and think about it,*
> *The further astray you wander from the truth.*
> *Stop talking and thinking*
> *And there is nothing that you will not be able*
> *to know.*

Stop knowing and not-knowing. Knowing is another kind of holding on, of separation; not-knowing is blank consciousness, emptiness. How do we avoid these extremes of form and emptiness, enlightenment and delusion? By learning to be ourselves, but not self-consciously, not passively. *Be serene in the oneness of things* does not mean "Watch the world go by" or "Do not do anything." That is not what Sozan is talking about, and it is not what our practice is. Being yourself means giving yourself permission to be who and what you are. That is "faith mind," having faith in your true self, trusting yourself. Until that happens, you cannot really trust anything or anybody. When you have that trust, your defensiveness disappears. You don't need to be arrogant or to put yourself down, to hide, or to withdraw. These two extremes are the same thing, different ways of protecting that idea of a separate self. Being yourself, being intimate with yourself, is the beginning of intimacy with all things. Being yourself is "no separation."

The Great Way is not difficult:
Direct word, direct speech.
In one, there are many phrases:
In two, there is one.
Difficult, difficult,
Picking and choosing, coming and going.
Be still, watch,
See for yourself.

> —From *Mountain Record of Zen Talks*
> by John Daido Loori.

Concluding Verse*

Let me respectfully remind you,
Life and death are of supreme importance.
Time swiftly passes by and opportunity
is lost.
Each of us should strive to awaken.
Awaken! Take heed, do not squander
your life.

---

*This verse is generally referred to as the *Evening Gatha*. *Gatha* is a short sutra that presents the dharma teachings in pithy wording, and this particular gatha is chanted in Zen monasteries at the end of each training day.

Glossary

C. = Chinese
J. = Japanese
S. = Sanskrit

BUDDHA (S.): A term that generally refers to an awakened being. The Buddha Shakyamuni specifically refers to Siddhartha Gautama, the founder of Buddhism who belonged to the Shakya clan of India.

DHARMA DISCOURSE (J. Teisho): A formal talk on a koan or on significant aspects of Zen teachings; not an intellectual presentation or a philosophical explanation, but a direct expression of the spirit of Zen by the teacher.

DIAMOND NET OF INDRA: An image from the Avatamsaka Sutra, pictured as a net with a jewel at each intersection. Each jewel reflects every other, graphically demonstrating the simultaneous mutual interdependence and intercausality of all things.

DOGEN KIGEN ZENJI: (1200–1253) Founder of the Japanese Soto School of Zen; Dogen established Eihei-ji, the principal Soto training monastery in Japan; he is the author of *Shobogenzo,* an important collection of dharma essays.

FAITH IN MIND SUTRA: A sutra on nonduality composed by Master Sengcan.

HARA (J.): The physical and spiritual center of one's body/mind; an area in the lower belly used in centering one's attention in meditation or any other activity.

JORIKI (J.): The power of concentration developed through the practice of meditation that allows practitioners to place their focus of attention where they choose (i.e., the breath, a koan) for extended periods of time.

KARMA (S.): The universal law of cause and effect, linking an action's underlying intention to that action's consequences; it equates the actions of the body, speech, and thought as potential sources of karmic consequences.

KI (J.; C. Chi): The vital life force present in and permeating all things; the energy that is the source of all creative activity.

KINHIN (J.): Walking meditation; it provides a transitional stage for shifting the concentration developed in zazen to activity.

KOAN (J.): An apparently paradoxical statement or question used in Zen training to induce in students an intense level of doubt that allows them to cut through conventional and conditioned descriptions of reality and see directly into their true nature.

SAMADHI (S.): The state in which the mind is absorbed in intense concentration, free from distractions and goals; the essential nature of the self can be experienced directly within samadhi.

SENGCAN (C.; J. Sozan): Died 606 C.E. He is regarded as the third ancestor of Chinese Zen, and is the author of the *Faith in Mind Sutra*.

SESSHIN (J.): "Gathering of the mind"; an extended period of intensive meditation practice that lasts between five and ten days.

SUTRA (S.): An important Buddhist text or scripture containing the teachings of Buddhism. Sutras often record the words attributed to Shakyamuni Buddha, or later Buddhist masters.

TEISHO (J.): See dharma discourse.

ZAFU (J.): A round pillow used in sitting meditation.

ZAZEN (J.): sitting meditation, which is taught in Zen as the most direct way to enlightenment; the practice of the realization of one's own true nature.

Suggested Reading List

Aitken, Robert, *Taking the Path of Zen* (San Francisco: North Point Press, 1982). A thorough introduction to Zen by one of the foremost American Zen teachers. Covers basic Zen teachings, including an emphasis on proper meditation practice.

Armstrong, Karen, *Buddha* (New York: Penguin, 2001). A short biography of the Buddha by a former Catholic nun. Uses the facts of the Buddha's life and analyzes his historical context to explain his teachings in a narrative format.

Beck, Charlotte Joko, *Everyday Zen: Love & Work* (San Francisco: Harper SanFrancisco, 1989). Sound advice on Zen practice in plain, accessible language from a prominent American Zen teacher. Encourages practitioners at all levels to include everything in their life as part of their practice.

Chödrön, Pema, *Start Where You Are* (Boston: Shambhala Publications, 1994). Instructions on compassion framed around fifty-nine traditional Tibetan Buddhist maxims. Provides basic Buddhist teachings and applies them to practicing in the twenty-first century.

Fields, Rick, *How the Swans Came to the Lake: A Narrative History of Buddhism in America* (Boston: Shambhala Publications, 1992). A seminal book that combines historical narrative with extensive references to Buddhist texts in order to trace the development of Buddhism in America. Includes sections on the role of women in Buddhism and social action.

Kapleau, Roshi Philip, ed., *The Three Pillars of Zen: Teaching, Practice, and Enlightenment* (New York: Anchor Books, 2000). A comprehensive overview of the history and discipline of Zen drawn from the author's experiences studying and translating for Japanese Zen masters. Includes detailed meditation instruction and actual transcripts from teacher-student interviews.

Loori, John Daido, ed., *The Art of Just Sitting: Essential Writings on the Zen Practice of Shikantaza* (Boston: Wisdom Publications, 2002). Explains the simple yet subtlest form of zazen practice, *shikantaza*. Includes essays by ancient and contemporary masters.

———. *The Eight Gates of Zen: A Program of Zen Training* (Boston: Shambhala Publications, 2002). Essential instructions on establishing a Zen practice, guided by Daido Roshi's unique American Zen training matrix. Explores how practice allows us to manifest wisdom and compassion in our everyday lives.

———. *Mountain Record of Zen Talks* (Mt. Tremper, N.Y.: Dharma Communications, 1988). A collection of talks investigating Zen practice as a spiritual journey of self-discovery. Begins with basic talks on zazen, progresses to discussions of how zazen leads to realizing the true nature of reality, and finally explores how to actualize these insights in our daily activities.

———. *Path of Enlightenment: Stages in a Spiritual Journey* (Mt. Tremper, N.Y.: Dharma Communications, 1999). Explains the ancient ox-herding pictures as a map for studying the self. Clarifies the ten phases of practice encountered on the path of realization.

———, ed., *Sitting with Koans* (Boston: Wisdom Publications, 2006). A collection of classic and modern writings on the meaning, history, and dynamics of koan practice. Includes commentaries by Chinese, Japanese, and American Zen masters.

Rahula, Walpola, *What the Buddha Taught* (New York: Grove Press, 1989). A scholar-monk's comprehensive, readable account of the Buddha's teachings on the Four Noble Truths.

Master Sheng-yen, *Getting the Buddha Mind,* ed. Ernest Heau (Elmhurst, N.Y.: Dharma Drum Publications, 1982). A compilation of lectures given by Ch'an Master Sheng-yen during retreats. Offers basic advice on practice as well as a sense of the atmosphere of a Ch'an retreat.

Suzuki, Shunryu, *Zen Mind, Beginner's Mind* (Trumbull, Conn.: Weatherhill, 2001). A classic explication of Zen practice from one of the first Zen teachers in America. Includes advice on posture and breathing, discipline and religion, and how to maintain basic motivation.

Photo Credits

Photographs appearing in this book are used courtesy of:

Robert Aichinger—page 45
Joel Sansho Benton—pages 13, 25, 36, 41, 87
Michael Joen—page 30
John Daido Loori—pages 54, 68, 74
National Buddhist Archive—pages 7, 15, 17, 19, 20, 22, 33, 58, 64, 92, 96
Matt Pokoik—page 80
Don Symanski—page 50

About Zen
Mountain Monastery

Zen Mountain Monastery is an American Zen Buddhist monastery and training center for monks and lay practitioners. It is located on a 230-acre site on Tremper Mountain in New York's Catskill Mountains, surrounded by state forest wilderness and featuring an environmental studies institute. The monastery provides a year-round daily training program that includes Zen meditation, various forms of face-to-face teaching, academic studies, liturgy, work practice, body practice, art practice, and study of the Buddhist precepts. Each month an introductory weekend Zen training workshop and a week-long silent Zen meditatation retreat (*sesshin*) are offered. During the spring and fall quarters of each year, ninety-day intensive programs are conducted. Throughout the year, the regular daily schedule is supplemented with seminars and workshops in the Zen arts, the martial arts, Buddhist studies, and other areas relevant to present-day Western practitioners. Students can train in either full-time or part-time residency or as nonresidents whose "home practice" is fueled by periodic visits to the monastery.

For further information, contact:

REGISTRAR
ZEN MOUNTAIN MONASTERY
P.O. BOX 197
871 SOUTH PLANK RD.
MOUNT TREMPER, N.Y. 12457
(845) 688-2228

registrar@mro.org

www.mrp.org

Library of Congress cataloging-in-publication data

Loori, John Daido.
Finding the Still Point: a beginner's guide to
Zen meditation/John Daido Loori.
p.   cm.
Originally published: The still point. Boston:
Dharma Communications, 1996.
Includes bibliographical references.
ISBN 978-1-59030-479-2 (pbk: alk. paper)
1. Meditation—Zen Buddhism. I. Loori, John Daido.
The still point. II. Title.
BQ9288.L663 2007
294.3'4435—dc22
2006051276